Throttle Up!
Teacher Astronaut Christa McAuliffe

By
Tom Patrick McAuliffe

Book #3 of 'The McAuliffe Series'

NEXT STOP PARADISE
PUBLISHING
Ft. Walton Beach, Florida, USA

Throttle Up!
Teacher Astronaut Christa McAuliffe
By Tom McAuliffe

Copyright © 2022

TABLE OF CONTENTS

<u>Dedication</u>

**To Christa and all those who push the boundaries
for the benefit of humankind *and*
*for guys like Steve who support them.***

100% of the Profits of this Book will be donated to
Challenger Centers
and
The Christa McAuliffe Center

"The crew of the space shuttle Challenger honored us by the manner in which they lived their lives. We will never forget them, nor the last time we saw them, this morning, as they prepared for their journey and waved goodbye and 'slipped the surly bonds of earth' to 'touch the face of God.'"
President Ronald Reagan
January 28, 1986

"The future of this country and the welfare of the free world depends upon our success in space. There is no room in this country for anything but a urgently motivated all-out effort toward space leadership."
President Lyndon Johnson, 1966

"We choose to go to the moon. We choose to go to the moon in this decade... and do the other things not because they are easy but because they are hard! The exploration of space will go ahead, whether we join in it or not."
President John F. Kennedy, 1962

COUNTDOWN

It was the 1950s, and America's paranoia about the Russians was at a fever pitch and knew no bounds. On October 4, 1957, Americans turned red, but it was a shade of embarrassment. News of a successful satellite launch by Russia left many Americans scratching their heads in disbelief. They were not used to feeling beaten in global competition or being in second place. Russia nicknamed it 'Sputnik One', and it immediately became the topic of conversation in homes from the Atlantic to the Pacific and back again."What about our space program?" Americans wanted to know. "How'd they get so far ahead of us?"

The USSR's launch pushed the United States space program and its public relations efforts were kicked into high gear, and within a year, the National Aeronautics and Space Administration (NASA) was formed, and President Eisenhower declared space exploration to be a top priority for America. Soon, the United States could boast of its own accomplishments above the Earth. Alan Shepard became the first American astronaut in space, spending a short 15 minutes and 22 seconds in flight on May 5, 1961.

Like thousands of American schoolchildren, young Christa Corrigan watched Shepard's brief flight with amazement on a black-and-white television in the school cafeteria."Someday, I'm going to ride in space!" she said. And her head was tilted towards the stars from that time on. Time raced on and before long it was the 1970s… the time of disco, afros, and bell bottoms. After she married Steve and became Mrs. McAuliffe, she became a teacher. Christa shared her own special interest in the space program with her children and her students, and in 1984 when President Ronald Reagan announced that NASA should search for the first civilian passenger in space and that it should also be a teacher... McAuliffe knew what she had to do. She immediately applied for the new 'Teacher in Space' program. On July 19, 1985, her dream became a reality when she was chosen to be the first teacher and US civilian to go on a space mission. Upon learning the news, Christa told reporters she was floating, and she wasn't sure when she was going to come back down to earth! She was smart, articulate, pretty, and she was able to make space fun and special again. She was perfect.

The story of Christa McAuliffe is more than the tale of a simple school girl who dreamed of going to space. It's a complex story about fate, setting goals, and working hard to achieve them, and it's also a story about trusting God and the talents he's giving you to make your and others' lives better. Sadly, it is also a story about greed, political pressure, and negligence.

Christa's dream ended on January 28, 1986, with the explosion of the Space Shuttle Challenger 73 seconds after launching from Pad 39a at the Cape in Florida. The world mourned her death, and there's little doubt that people will continue to look back on that historic date with sadness and sometimes anger. It was indeed traumatizing for the nation.

But as we remember the tragic death of Christa, it's vital to also remember her life. She lived with a zest for life and shared her energy, talents, and knowledge unselfishly. Christa cared about people, all sorts of people: students, neighbors, friends, strangers.

After her death, the courageous educator received the Congressional Medal of Honor for Space. But that was just a sample of the proper honors bestowed upon her. For example, as a tribute to her memory, an asteroid and a crater on the moon were named after her. In addition, there are now numerous elementary, junior, and senior high schools that bear this name. Additionally, the Christa McAuliffe Center at Framingham State College was established to carry on her legacy and support the advancement of innovative education throughout the nation.

This book is about Christa's life, and the author shall not go into all the media optics and politics involved in the loss of these brave people and a taxpayer-funded multi-billion dollar spacecraft. However, it is important to note that many believe this was not an 'accident' at all but was predicted and an eventuality. There's enough blame to go around, but research reveals two important facts:

One is that the Reagan administration, desperately needing some positive news after being involved in significant scandals, did exert pressure on NASA to have the Shuttle in space so that the President could talk with them or refer to them during his State of the Union speech before Congress, slated for the 28th, the date of the launch. The overall NASA goal was to make spaceflight a regular occurrence and to make living and working in space a realistic goal.

The second undeniable fact is that the manufacturer of the Solid Rocket Booster, Morton Thiokol of Utah, knew of and warned NASA about how the"O" rings (which seal the rocket and prevent the venting of fuel) would react to freezing temperatures. Pressure to stay on schedule resulted in 'Go Fever'.

To date, Morton Thiokol and NASA have yet to be charged for their criminal negligence. No one has been held accountable. The final report from the Congressional Rogers Commission, set up to 'investigate' the 'Accident', was seen as nothing more than a political whitewash and not a real effort to find the truth. We will probably never know the full story. In 2011, the United States discontinued the Space Shuttle program, but the legacy of Astronaut Teacher Christa McAuliffe lives on! This is her story.

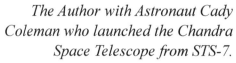

Fall 2022

The Author with Astronaut Cady Coleman who launched the Chandra Space Telescope from STS-7.

CHAPTER 1

Growing Up

*"Exploration really is the essence of the human spirit,
and to pause, to falter, to turn our back on the quest for
knowledge, is to perish."*
NASA Astronaut Frank Borman

"Where there is no vision, the people perish."
Proverbs 29:18

Her eyes widened, and the 13-year-old stared at the paper she held in her hands. She couldn't believe what she saw. "Sharon Christa Corrigan", the puzzled girl shook her head. Who was that!?

For a moment, Christa even thought about running back to the Rectory and asking the Nun if there had been some sort of mistake. The year was 1961, and like thousands of other eighth graders across the country, she was preparing for her confirmation. She was Catholic. It was when she stopped by the Rectory, a place where priests and nuns live, to pick up her required baptismal certificate that she made the surprising discovery. Her name was not what she had always known. The name on her baptismal certificate was not right, so she rushed home to find out why.

Her parents quickly cleared up the confusion... It seems that when Christa, or rather "Sharon Christa", was born on September 2, 1948, both her parents were expecting a boy. They were all set to name their new son

"Christopher", reflecting pride in the Scottish-Irish tradition of their ancestry, but when the baby turned out to be a precious girl, Ed and Grace Corrigan had to change their plans. So they scanned the book of names carefully, weighing each possibility, and came across "Sharon". Because "Christa" was the feminine form of "Christopher," the new member of the Corrigan family was christened Sharon Christa Corrigan.

However, within a few weeks, the family began calling the baby 'Sharon Christa'… but soon the Sharon disappeared when her brown hair turned blonde and she took on a Scandinavian look, at least according to Mr. Corrigan. The firstborn of the Corrigan family called herself Christa, and so did everyone else. Whenever she needed a middle name, she simply made one up; sometimes it was Mary, other times it was Carol and sometimes even Georgie, making up different names to suit different occasions.

 But it was not until she was ready to be confirmed in the Catholic Church that she found out the whole truth. Her real name was... Sharon Christa Corrigan. It didn't seem quite fair to totally ignore the Sharon in her name, but after years of being Christa, it was a bit late to change.

Not that Christa Corrigan needed a unique name to be considered special. Her early years were filled with unusual adventures and achievements that set her apart. As a young child, Christa developed bronchitis, causing Mr. and Mrs. Corrigan to travel often to Children's Hospital in Boston, Massachusetts. Once the problems disappeared, it was problems with her intestines that ravaged the young girl, and she underwent 28 straight days of intravenous feeding. After battling to survive, an antibiotic finally conquered the disease.

From then on, young Christa was a quick learner. She listened to everyone around her, echoing their words and repeating them back in complete sentences. She could talk at 16 months, and she was already reciting nursery rhymes! While her dad, Ed Corrigan, attended accounting classes, his wife stayed home and tended to the baby. They both watched the family budget. The Corrigans had to stretch every penny. In their 2nd floor flat on Columbia Avenue, just outside of Boston, their

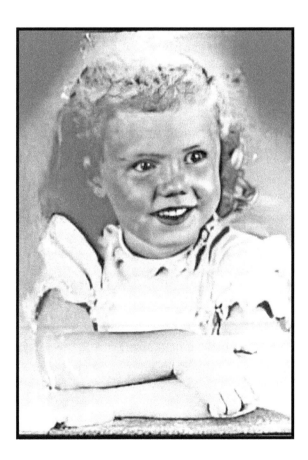

only luxury was a tiny dog named "Teddy". Soon, the dog became Christa's favorite playmate, and the lovable pet proved to be a lifesaver... literally.

Grass or a lawn was a rarity in the

15

housing project the Corrigan family lived in. It was surrounded by cement pavement. Almost every time little Christa started to wander off with Teddy, Mrs. Corrigan came running. One day, the little girl pedaled her tricycle up the block to a major intersection in the neighborhood with cars zipping and zooming by in every direction. Little Christa was paying them no attention whatsoever. Suddenly came Teddy, running and jumping along the path and barking an alarm as loud as he could. A few people, including one of the Corrigan's neighbors, noticed the little girl on her tricycle near the roadway. Meanwhile, Teddy raced to the street, snagging the little girl's long-legged pants and dragging her towards the sidewalk! The neighbor finally got there and helped pull little Christa out of harm's way. Thankfully, her daughter's guardian angel kept her safe that day, Mrs. Corrigan would later remark. But Teddy helped too.

The Corrigan family grew steadily as they welcomed brothers Christopher and Steven and then two sisters, Betsy and Lisa, to the clan. Christa, desperate to please, enjoyed following her mother around, eagerly volunteering to do the slightest task. Once in school, Christa quickly learned reading and writing. She attended Brookwater Elementary in Framingham, Massachusetts, and spent many hours improving her handwriting. She wanted to be the best at whatever she did and saw no reason why she couldn't be.

As time progressed, Mr. Corrigan proved himself as an able accountant, while Mrs. Corrigan set out to be the best housewife and mother possible. Christa's mom taught nursery school and organized a Brownie troop. If one of her children showed an interest in singing, voice lessons were somehow lined up. Dancing and piano lessons became regular items on the schedule despite the family budget. The only thing tighter than the budget was the living arrangements, with 7 family members living in a 3 bedroom home. One thing was sure: the children always came first.

Despite two prominent front teeth that prompted the other kids to call her "Chipmunk," Christa won special attention because of her smooth skin, sparkly brown eyes, and soft auburn hair, which was worn in pigtails. She was indeed the wholesome girl-next-door and the epitome of cute. She even modeled young girls' clothing for a local department store and was elected 'Summer

Princess' at an annual neighborhood event. She was a good kid who loved her parents and her life. Whenever teachers required Christa to write about the person she most admired, it was no easy choice, and so she alternated between writing about her father or her mother. In each case, Christa always felt she had plenty of material to work with.

In her eyes, Ed Corrigan was the perfect dad. It wasn't that he was so good at his job; it was that he always found time for his kids. Although she was the oldest of the five Corrigan kids, she knew she was "daddy's little girl", and she loved the label. As Mr. Corrigan's fingers slipped over the ivory keys of the baby grand piano in the family living room, Christa stood nearby and sang. She cheerfully obeyed her dad's request to sing before friends and visitors. At the annual local talent show, Christa was onstage, sharing her gifts and soaking up the applause. She "might be another Judy Garland," Mr. Corrigan would boast, but he never pushed Christa into anything she didn't want to do, and besides, she was a natural.

Christa never ceased to marvel at her mom's ability to get a million things done at once. With a smile that had enough power to light a small city, she made sure that each of her five children always had clean outfits ready to go. The clothes might not be new, but they were always clean. It all required a rare talent for juggling time, schedules, and tasks. If one child came down with the flu, the rest would follow, and then there was always the refereeing of squabbles and disputes. It was, in general, a busy and happy home.

The Corrigans did things as a family as often as possible. For example, New Year's Eve called for an annual dinner at a favorite local seafood restaurant. Summer brought short family vacations to Cape Cod and the Great Lakes.

"We couldn't afford to stay long at any one place," Christa recalled. "But we made the most of the time we spent together. Sure, we kids fought, but it was never for long. Mom and Dad helped us realize that the time spent being mad was just wasted time."

It was a valuable lesson. Every moment counted in the Corrigan house. On Sunday mornings, Mr. Corrigan was a stickler about making it to Mass, and anyone who didn't make it would pay the consequences. Each of his children learned their prayers, and he enjoyed hearing them recited out loud. Christa seldom disappointed her parents with her prayers or anything else. Her schoolwork reflected quality and dedication. She routinely received A's in most of her classes and took pride in any extra credit activities.

On May 5, 1961, Christa sat in the school cafeteria watching a small black-and-white TV at Lincoln Junior High. Her eyes wide, she and her classmates watched American astronaut Alan Shepard blast off into space and stay there for more than 15 minutes! She scribbled in her notebook, capturing the historical event and her reactions to it. Christa told her friends,"I'm going to ride in space someday!" Soon afterward, President Kennedy announced that the United States would have a man on the Moon by the end of the decade, and a program was put in place to make that dream a reality.

These were exciting times filled with opportunities for achievement in space. And for many in the student cafeteria, including Christa Corrigan, the idea of living and working in space didn't sound impossible at all. While some shook their heads, others set about the work of getting it done.

Christa took note. "I can remember in early elementary school when the Russians launched the first satellite. There was still so much unknown about space," she would recall years later. "People thought Mars was probably populated!"

The future was bright with possibility and innovation, and while President Kennedy spoke of a "man" on the Moon, the time hadn't yet come for people to consider a woman for such a mission, and the precocious young lady Christa Corrigan didn't think that was fair. But that summer, when she went to the annual fair, heading off into space was the furthest thing from her mind... she got sick just riding on the Ferris wheel!

CHAPTER 2

Schoolin'

"Tell me and I forget. Teach me and I remember. Involve me and I learn."
Benjamin Franklin

"If you are planning for a year, sow rice; if you are planning for a decade, plant trees; if you are planning for a lifetime… educate people."
Chinese Proverb

In the fall of 1961, Marian High School was a different world for Christa Corrigan. Her teachers were Catholic nuns, wearing long black 'habits' and starched white bibs. They looked a little like tuxedoed penguins. Not only did they teach English, math, history, and science, but they charged their students to lift their souls and minds to God. The students wore uniforms, and like the other girls, Christa wore white blouses tucked into plaid skirts with a gray vest and blue blazer. Boys wore blue dress shirts, black ties, and dark or khaki pants with navy blue jackets. Naturally, public school kids made fun of them.

Christa wasted no time at her new high school. She had someplace to go. She was not sure where, but she had an urgency to move forward and get there. Her academics were important, but she also jumped into extracurricular activities in a big way. She enjoyed singing, acting, and performing in musicals. She also played in the orchestra, was elected to the Student Council, and when she wasn't shooting basketballs on the gym floor, she was pounding out home runs and running bases outside on the softball field!

Like so many teenagers, Christa sometimes found herself fantasizing about her future; a trip to the movies and it was dreams of becoming a movie star. Christa chuckled and imagined herself as a female Inspector Clouseau. If she went to a big-name concert she then considered becoming a major recording artist. In other moments of reflection, she thought about becoming a nun, imagining herself wearing a large crucifix worn by the sisters at Marian High. The future was full of possibilities.

When Steve McAuliffe entered her life during Christa's sophomore year at Marian, it was for good, although neither realized it at the time. She immediately recognized his assertiveness and enthusiasm, but Steve was tongue-tied when it came to girls, especially Christa. The two of them shared a homeroom class together, but only looks from across the room were exchanged. It took months before they began talking to each other, but once they started, they seemingly couldn't stop. Christa and Steve showed up at dances and sporting events together, yet they loved to be joined by their friends."Christa was always on the lookout for a way to touch the lives of other people," observed one high school friend. "When a new kid entered Marion High, Christa was always among the first to make the newcomer feel welcome... it was just the way she was," they said. Indeed.

In her Girl Scout troop and in church activities, Christa displayed the same kind of unselfish friendliness and leadership. "I never felt good about myself if I wasn't giving," Christa observed. "I felt like I was cheating myself and everyone else I had a chance to help." It was never enough for her to just join a group; Christa had to

fully participate. She never wanted to miss seeing the Marion Mustangs play football, and in theater, she loved performing on stage. One of her favorite roles was Sister Margarita in 'The Sound of Music'. But her studies always came first. The classroom didn't always come that easily for her, however. She enjoyed taking courses that challenged her, with social studies classes proving to be especially exciting. She loved history, and there certainly was a lot of that in New England. Christa sometimes daydreamed about what it must've been like to be a colonialist fighting for independence at the birth of our nation. Abigail Adams, the wife of the outspoken president John Adams, became a personal heroine and inspiration for McAuliffe.

"She had spirit and spunk," Christa wrote in an essay about the dynamic First Lady."At a time when most women were docile and silent, Abigail Adams fought her own battle for independence, showing her husband and others that a woman was something more than just a baby bearer. She was informed and spoke out on the issues of the day. She was a woman who was her own person and really a force to be reckoned with," she said.

Christa worked on balancing her schedule between schoolwork and extracurricular activities, and the

struggle paid off; she was elected to the National Honor Society in recognition of her good grades and contributions to her school. In spite of her busy schedule at Marion High, Christa still found time to spend with her family. "She's born to babysit," her father observed. "First she watched her own brothers and sisters… then she branched out to watch everybody else's kids! All of our friends knew they could leave their kids with Christa and never have to worry about them," he said.

Christa saved her babysitting money for College. During the summers she found other odd jobs and Steve was never too far away. When she gave swimming lessons at a local lake, Steve was the lifeguard. When she worked the counter for a dry cleaners… Steve made the deliveries. Reluctantly Christa followed her parents advice and tried dating other boys but it just didn't work out. She knew Steve was the one for her at 16 and the two of them talked about spending their lives together. But all that would need to come after college and they promised their parents they would wait.

In the winter of 1963 Christa read about the annual Girl Scout Roundup, scheduled for the next summer in Idaho. Never having been away from home Christa set out to win a free trip to the Roundup. She knew it wouldn't be easy but she felt ready for the challenge and during the next six months, she filled out countless forms and wrote many essays to win money for the trip. "What kind of leader am I?", "What are my rights and responsibilities as an American citizen?" "How has the History of our country effected you?"

Christa had to ask herself these questions and come up with well-thought-out essay answers. It was a great exercise in logic and writing and it laid a good groundwork for what was to come later.

For the Girl Scouts, she also had to perform other tasks like pitching a tent in under three minutes, testing her agility, and administering first aid and CPR, showing how she could react in emergency situations. She also had to demonstrate various survival skills, and she attended seminars and lectures, scribbling notes as well as writing reports.

Judges interviewed her, testing her powers of observation and her ability to think on her feet. She did well. Christa's efforts paid off, and in July 1964, she boarded the train for the week-long trip to Idaho with hundreds of other Girl Scouts from all over the USA. Out west, Christa enjoyed seven days of camping, canoeing, and making new friends. It was an experience she'd never forget. She realized that there was a large world out there.

As a senior at Marion High School, Christa knew it was time to make many important decisions. There was no doubt that whatever plan she devised would have to include Steve. But even with a possible marriage, she sincerely wanted to carve out her own niche and make her own personal contribution to the big world out there. But she wondered how she would make her mark and in what profession.

CHAPTER 3

Young Love

*"And in the end, the love you take
is equal to the love you make."*
The Beatles,"The End"

*"Love is a lot like a backache. It doesn't show up on X-
Rays but you know it's there."*
George Burns, comedian and actor

If anyone thought Christa Corrigan would slow down
her hectic pace when she reached college, they were
sadly mistaken. She enrolled at Framingham State
College in the fall of 1968, choosing courses that would
lead to a degree in American History. Her classes in high
school were a major influence on Christa's life. Not only
did she develop a love for history and social studies, she
also decided that she wanted to be... a teacher! At the
time, she did not realize what a momentous decision for
her life that would turn out to be.

In addition to a full class load at Framingham College,
Christa joined the Debate Team and the Glee Club. She
was eager to pay her own expenses, so she also took a
job working nights as a clerk at a local trucking
company. Meanwhile, she found time to babysit
whenever possible and did whatever she could to make
and save money. But gone were the nightly phone calls
and weekend dates with Steve, who was 600 miles away
at Virginia Military Institute. The two nonviolent

of them decided that being separated would test their
true feelings for one another. The separation would
help them know if, indeed, marriage was in their
future. It did.

Christa was not the only Corrigan who ever attended
Framingham State, because in the fall of '68, her
mother decided to take art classes at the college.
Together in an old Volkswagen, they shared the five-
minute drive from home to campus and back again,
and the rides were seldom quiet. Both Christa and
Grace Corrigan enjoyed being college coeds, and the
generation gap between them disappeared as they
chatted the miles away during the commute.

College life changed Christa. She found herself
becoming more aware of the world around her and
seeking a place in it where she could make a true
difference. American soldiers continued to fight and
die in Vietnam, while back in the States, people,
especially students, grew more and more disenchanted
with the conflict. The death toll of American soldiers
climbed to more than 2500 a month, and hospital
planes carried home soldiers who were severely
injured both physically and mentally.

Across the country, college students protested against
the continued fighting, and like so many of her peers,
Christa deplored the war in Southeast Asia. At home,
Dr. Martin Luther King would alert her to the long and
hard struggle for equal human rights, and when he fell
victim to an assassin's bullet in 1968, she was
devastated. MLK's constant call for peaceful,

action in seeking civil rights spoke to her. With discontent in many black neighborhoods and riots in major American cities, President Lyndon Johnson struggled to bring order. When Senator Robert Kennedy of New York was also shot and killed only two months later, she was full of despair over the bleakness of America's future. It was a sad time for her, for our nation, for everyone.

The U.S. space program brought a sense of hope to Americans from coast to coast. NASA's successes were a welcome relief from the troubles in Vietnam and on the streets of our country. As she sat in a history course that covered the expansion of the American frontier, Christa thrilled at the stories of the brave and adventurous souls who risked their lives to begin a new life in the American west. Yet, with all those mountains and deserts now explored, she wondered if there were any worlds left that still needed to be discovered. "Would any of you be willing to go to the Moon if you had a chance?" Christa's instructor asked one day in class. There was no hesitation, and Christa's hand shot up! If they were no longer frontiers to be challenged on the Earth, it was only natural to seek them elsewhere, and she began to think about that.

Apollo Astronauts Frank Borman and James Lovell addressed the Earth from circling the Moon on Christmas Eve 1968, showing our planet from a new, out-of-this-world perspective. It had a profound effect on many, including Christa. As Borman read the opening passage from the Bible, "In the beginning God created the heavens and the earth...", the biblical account of the creation of the world was being broadcast to a home more than 238,000 miles away.

It was a special moment for humanity, and it had a real impact on the young couple. People began to have a more global perspective and came to realize how fragile our planet is. A little less than a year later, as Christa and Steve drove on a vacation trip, their car radio relayed news of the Apollo mission and men landing on the Moon.

As the Astronauts transmitted from the Sea of Tranquility on the Moon, "That's one small step for man, one giant leap for mankind," the young lovers could not have felt more positive about the future. It was a welcome relief from the troubles of the time.

Then Armstrong became the first person to set foot on the Moon, and the prediction of JFK that America would place a man on the Moon by the end of the decade had come true! Like millions of Americans, Christa felt a renewed pride in our country. The public conjecture was that it would not be long before space travel was commonplace and we would have settlements on the Moon. In fact, Eastern Airlines issued announcements about the first commercial flight to the Moon... Christa and Steve signed up.

When the young men at Framingham State suggested dinner and a movie, Christa smiled, "I'm seeing someone," she would answer politely, "but thanks for asking." Dating Steve at every opportunity, Christa would make the drive to VMI every few weeks and some weekends. The two of them spent much of their time just walking. Steve was frequently challenging his teachers or others in authority, resulting in Saturday detentions. The walking excursions were not particularly exciting, but they gave the couple a valuable chance to talk and make plans for the future. They fell deeply in love.

As Christa made plans for her future, she also became more socially involved and evolved. She supported the women's rights movement and the Equal Rights Amendment. "There should never be any door shut in someone's face because of his or her sex," she said. Feminist speakers visiting the college often found Christa in the front row.

She was also all about standing up for the rights of both black and Native Americans, insisting that the United States government "allow no prejudice or bigotry to hold any citizen back from the pursuit of his or her rights." At the time, some felt her views were a little too radical, but they knew her heart was in the right place and that she cared about her students, the country and the future.

As Christa found her attitudes changing and deepening, she enjoyed expressing her uniqueness. In a sign of the times, her outward appearance changed, and she now had a bleached Afro hairdo, along with her bright patterned dresses, horn-rimmed glasses, and a dramatic, eye-catching shade of white lipstick. Psychedelic! She loved rock and roll, but drugs were out of the question. Unlike many young people in the late 60s, the closest Christa ever came to pot or cocaine was to read about them. She wanted nothing to do with drugs – she was way too busy with life.

As the leader of a local Girl Scout troop, Christa also saw herself as somewhat of a role model. She led her troop to Washington, DC, where they roamed through the Smithsonian Institute, visited the Tomb of the Unknown Soldier, and stopped by the White House tour. It was an impactful trip, and she would recall many years later that it was one of the first times in her life that she could recall truly being on her own. New Hampshire also beckoned with its snowy hills for skiing, forests for camp outs and picnics, all part of a fun-filled scouting program.

"I got so much out of being a Girl Scout," said Christa. "I just wanted to help others do the same." After completing her work at Framingham State, Christa displayed a final reflection of her convictions at her graduation ceremony. Like many of her classmates, she wore a black armband as a visual protest against the Vietnam war. It was noticed.

As her bachelor's diploma was safely tucked under her arm, Christa started to focus on new plans for her life. She knew three important things: she was not done with becoming educated (in fact, she received a Masters of Education at Bowie State College in 1978), she sincerely wanted to become a teacher, and she truly loved Steve. August 23, 1970, would be the day of her next big step.

CHAPTER 4

Mrs. Teacher

"If I can get some student interested in science, if I can show members of the general public what's going on up there in the space program, then my job's been done. This opportunity to connect my abilities as an educator with my interests in history and space is a unique opportunity to fulfill my early fantasies."
Christa McAuliffe

"Education is the most powerful weapon which you can use to change the world."
Nelson Mandela

"Are you sure you want your wedding on a Sunday?"
"Have you thought about the music?"
"Will there be a reception?"
So many questions! From the moment Christa graduated from Framingham State, all her attention refocused. For seven years, she had dated Steve McAuliffe... There had never been really any other man in her life, and now they were going to head down the aisle and get married. "I never realized how much work goes into a wedding," she admitted during the summer of 1970. "The guys have it so easy!" The preparation for the big day was ongoing, and only one detail proved beyond her control... the weather.

A steady drizzle greeted the wedding guests as they arrived at the Catholic Church early in the afternoon of

August 23rd. Inside the church, people greeted each other with friendly nods, warm hugs, and solid handshakes. The site and time of 21-year-old Christa Corrigan's wedding day had arrived. With daisies in her hair, the beautiful bride raised a loving murmur as she drifted down the aisle on her father's arm. She was a sight to behold, and at the end of the aisle was her high school sweetheart, Steve McAuliffe.

"She had always looked good to me," said Steve, "but on our wedding day, Christa looked truly like an angel from heaven." With Steve's brother Wayne serving as the Best Man and a close friend of Christa's as Maid of Honor, they became husband and wife.

From the church, it was on to a reception in the Corrigan's backyard with hundreds of well-wishers jamming to the rock 'n' roll music of a local band, enjoying food and drink while wishing the new Mr. and Mrs. McAuliffe all the best. Christa, ever the perfect host, went from group to group, sharing her thanks and never losing her smile. By dusk, most of the wedding guests had departed, and the newlyweds

rolled away in an aging VW bug with a trailer filled with gifts. Following behind them was the sound of tin cans tied to the back fender, indicating they were… "Just Married!"

Most newlyweds enjoy a week or two of honeymoon, but not this couple. It was Sunday night, and Steve was scheduled to start classes at Georgetown University Law School first thing Tuesday morning. Nope, there would be no honeymoon in Hawaii or Florida for this couple.

Perhaps another time. For the time being, it was important to get settled into an elbow-to-elbow apartment in Washington, DC.

The new apartment came fully furnished and even had running water when the roof leaked! It also featured built-in house guests... according to Christa, the roaches were bigger than the furniture.

Fortunately, the new Mrs. McAuliffe immediately started a job as a substitute teacher at a local junior high school. She decided that it felt good to sit behind the biggest desk in the room. As the new wife and teacher traced the history of America for her eighth-grade students, from the pilgrims and the colonists to all the presidents of American history, she wanted to ensure it all came to life in "Mrs. M's" classroom.

In their tiny apartment at night, the newlyweds sat around their simple kitchen table, and because they had no extra money to splurge on restaurants or movies, they simply enjoyed each other's company instead. They always had. It was a special but stressful time as they got a start on their life together. Christa would be

grading reports and tests while Steve would be deep into his tax law books, which were about a foot thick and weighed a as much as a small car.

"Some might think we suffered," Christa recalled, "but when you're as much in love as we were... everything's fine."

In the fall of 1971, Christa's teaching assignment changed, and she found a new and permanent position in Maryland, only 15 minutes away. In addition to history, English and civics were added to her teaching load at Thomas Jefferson Junior High School. One thing was certain: her new students presented a far greater challenge in terms of teaching and learning. Many of her new students were African American and came from broken and troubled homes.

Although she was not a counselor, Mrs. McAuliffe found herself listening to her young people before and after school. Many suffered abuse within their families and faced the dangers of the street every day. "It's awfully hard to get a child interested in nouns and verbs or the Declaration of Independence when they're hungry or worried about getting beat up at home or killed on the way to school," Christa said.

Someone must've told officials of Johnson Junior High School how effectively Christa handled living in small quarters because she found herself in equally close classrooms at work. Overcrowding in the school had forced her to convert a corner of the school library into her classroom. Time Magazine covers filled the walls of her makeshift classroom, and she made the most of a small temporary chalkboard. Her talent for guitar playing delighted her students as they learned how America grew not only through reading about historical events but also through music. Songs like "America the Beautiful" and "This Land is Your Land" had Christa strumming her way through the textbooks as her kids sang along. It was a great way to reach them and get them involved in the learning material. It proved to be a very effective teaching method and she used it throughout her career.

Despite their proximity to many famous locations in the nation's capital, most students at Jefferson had never traveled outside their own neighborhood. Teacher McAuliffe changed all that. She set up field trips to the first permanent English settlement in the New World, "Jamestown", and buses full of students also visited Gettysburg, Pennsylvania, where a major Civil War battle took place, and President Abraham Lincoln gave his famous address in 1863. There were other trips as well, sometimes to courtrooms to watch the justice system at work first-hand or to the prisons where they met those most directly touched by the same system. For her, the world was her classroom and getting students to fully engage and actually feel history in a real and lasting way was the goal and she was willing to try anything to reach them.

"Mrs. McAuliffe gave us so much," Student Yolanda Jackson recalled. "A lot of us didn't have many bright spots in our lives, so we looked forward to school and Mrs. McAuliffe's class. We didn't just read about history and stuff, we saw where it really happened. She wasn't just a teacher, she was our friend," Yolanda said fondly recalling her teacher.

Christmas season 1972 saw a cat named Rizzo join the family, purring his way into Christa's and Steve's hearts as well as a new and larger apartment. Their home became a refuge from the tremulous times outside. In

January 1974, national integration laws went into effect, moving thousands of black students in the United States to previously all-white schools. Many notable minority leaders said the move was long overdue. Those directly affected, the black and white students, felt frightened and uncomfortable, but Christa did everything she could to ease the situation. For the boys and girls of Johnson who had to change schools, she had folders prepared with each student's name on them. Inside, she included a small personal note of encouragement. She even contacted the new teachers of her students, explaining each student's strengths and weaknesses. It was surprising to fellow teachers and students alike.

The year 1976 was special for America; it was the 200th anniversary of the nation. Bicentennial observances were planned across the country, and in McAuliffe's hometown of Concord, New Hampshire, it was no different. Christa and Steve looked forward to a special and personal way of observing the birth of their nation... The birth of their very first baby! "Just like a history teacher," Steve laughed. "She's always wanting to make a little history of her own!" Christa decided to start keeping a diary she could someday turn over to her children. She was a history teacher through and through.

Determined to raise the healthiest and happiest baby ever known, Christa read almost every book available about what a new mother should do. During her long pregnancy, she watched her diet and got plenty of exercise and sleep. This baby was God's gift, and Christa just wanted to make sure that nothing was going to go wrong.

The cry of a new baby boy filled the delivery room on September 11, 1976, as Scott McAuliffe made his entrance into the world. Mom and baby did well, and by mid-afternoon, all three McAuliffes were seated in the hospital room, watching the football game on TV. "Be proud that on your very first day on this earth, you watched the Washington Redskins beat the Chicago Bears!" Steve whispered to his new son and then wrote it in Scott's baby book.

During the summer of 1976, they watched many bicentennial celebrations on television. Christa tired easily while pregnant, and she relished the opportunity to watch history unfold on TV. The coverage of the past space missions was eagerly watched, and sometimes she would doze off and dream. She awoke with a start every now and then, smiling as she realized she had been dreaming of becoming an astronaut... she, Christa McAuliffe, in space? What a crazy notion!

CHAPTER 5

STS-51L 'Teacher in Space'

"The aeroplane will never fly."
Lord Haldane, Minister of War, Britain, 1907
(A statement made four years after Kitty Hawk.)

"With the Teacher in Space program NASA picked a public school teacher to go into space, observe and make a journal about the space flight, and I am a teacher who always dreamed of going up into space."
Christa McAuliffe

Christa thrived on being a mother, and her past experience with four younger brothers and a sister, as well as all the babysitting gigs, had prepared her well. But having your very own baby… well, that was completely different. It was special. "I thank God every day for letting me become a mother," she said, "and I also pray that he'll help me be a good mother."

When Steve accepted the job with the New Hampshire Attorney General's office the McAuliffe family headed back to Concord, New Hampshire. Although they returned during the blizzard of 1978, Christa felt very glad to be back at home.

Home to the McAuliffe's was now a classic three-story Victorian home on Concord Hill. Shingles covered the structure like an aged skin, and the roof and inside walls creaked in the wind. It was easy to see that the building had witnessed a lot of history -- a thought that didn't and couldn't go unnoticed. Christa always loved hearing stories about the old house.

While it needed repairs, the prospect of renovation didn't deter its new owners. "When you create something new out of something old, you become a part of it," Christa observed. In early 1979, Christa learned she was pregnant again and that the baby was due to arrive in August.

A beautiful healthy baby girl arrived a day after their ninth wedding anniversary. This time around, Christa had a real reason to pray for tiny Caroline McAuliffe. The infant, named after President Kennedy's first daughter, had some initial health challenges. Things turned out fine.

Even though money was tight, Steve and Christa purchased the newborn a tiny gold cross and chain to protect her. They watched every penny, seldom spending any money on themselves. They both found joy in their kids, spending hours reading, listening, and playing games with them.

 Making sure her own children were carefully supervised and cared for, Christa was ready to return to the classroom, and in the fall of 1980, she did. It was a welcome change, and she taught English and Social Studies at Rundlett Junior High in Concord, New Hampshire.

The following year, she transferred to Bow Memorial School, and as well as teaching the usual History and Civics classes, she developed a new class offering called 'The American Woman'.

"It has always seemed to me that women receive too little attention in the entire story of America," Christa asserted. "It was the men who were the soldiers, the statesman, the inventors, and all the rest… many times, if it hadn't been for mothers and wives, those very men would not have been free to make their contributions. It was the ordinary people as well as the leaders who made this nation great, and that certainly includes women," she said.

Many of these women kept journals which are useful in providing historical accounts of their times. Christa had kept one for years, and she also encouraged her students to keep a daily journal of their activities and feelings. Her peers respected her leadership, and they chose her to lead the local Teachers Union. Her date book was crowded with meetings as she fought for better conditions and wages for teachers. They usually received them through negotiation versus striking.

Alongside her roles as wife, mother, and teacher, Christa taught religion classes to eighth graders at Saint Peter's Catholic Church, getting them ready for their religious confirmation. When asked to be a Girl Scout troop leader again… how could Christa refuse because scouting had been such an important part of her own childhood? Then the call would come,"Will you join the Concord Junior Service League?" How could Christa say no? The CJSL offered scholarships to young women who were going to college! "We need volunteers to help raise funds for the Concord YMCA. Can you help?" "Of course!" came the answer. Christa McAuliffe did it all and seldom said no. How she managed to fulfill all of her many local responsibilities and raise two smart and polite kids at the same time was a small miracle. When she could, she would squeeze in time to play volleyball, tennis, or ski on the local slopes, but she was equally content just spending hours reading or at a sewing machine.

Students considering teaching as a career got special attention from Christa. And not in the form of extra credit or brownie points: she wanted those going into the education profession in the future to have a full and complete understanding of the field. She was always willing to linger after school sharing her insights with anyone seeking her counsel. "I don't teach social studies. I teach the future!" She said.

She truly enjoyed impacting and enriching the lives of others. For example, her habit of keeping journals and recommending doing so caught on at Bow High School, not only in Christa's classes but in others as well. So on April 12, 1981, many students were busy writing as they witnessed two Astronauts, John Young and Robert Crippin, circle the Earth for 54 hours in the new shuttle orbiter 'Columbia'. McAuliffe and her students didn't know that she was going to be following in those footsteps and in the near future.

Christa was proud of her work at Bow High School,

and when the Assistant Principal position opened up, she applied and felt she had a good chance. She didn't get the promotion, and in her mind, one of the reasons was that the school board administration was not really ready for a woman in a position of authority. The rejection saddened Christa, and she decided to move on. When a slot opened up at the local High School, Christa applied and was hired in the fall of 1982. Concord High School was highly regarded and respected, and also importantly, it was only three blocks away from the McAuliffe homestead… it was within walking distance!

It didn't take long for Christa to get comfortable in her new job at Concord High. In Classroom 305, students examined and debated the events of the day. Displays of recent newspaper clippings and magazine covers covered classroom bulletin boards. Over the months and years, she added to her list of teaching ideas and techniques. No one ever accused Mrs. McAuliffe of not being a creative teacher. And not all of the experiences came from textbooks; Christa brought in speakers and took her classes to hear speakers at local venues. She apologized to other teachers when her students would arrive late to other classes because of the field trips.

"But you should've heard what we heard! Groups of students acted out decades of history dressed as people of the time," McAuliffe explained. "I was Churchill and gave that speech about blood, sweat, and tears!" one student would volunteer. "Well, when we do the 1950s, I want to be Elvis!" another student offered.

The kids wrote skits and performed them, developing their writing and speaking skills as they learned about American history. Most importantly to Christa, students were fully involved and engrossed in learning. And for the young teacher, that was what it was all about.

In her high school law classes, cases and ideas went to trial in a courtroom-like atmosphere with students selected to be on both sides of whatever was being adjudicated. Steve, now in private law practice after four years with the state attorney's office, always took time out to share his opinions and law expertise.

Of all the special teaching techniques Christa used, she especially enjoyed it when students re-enacted past space missions. NASA's latest mission of shuttle Columbia was not the most dramatic, but it emphasized how common space travel was becoming. Launching, working in space, and then setting the craft down out in the California desert, ready to be used again, was becoming commonplace. "It won't be that much longer before families will be living and working in space!" said Astronaut Young.

Comments like that stirred up Christa's old yearnings, and she remembered watching Alan Shepard blasting off into space back in 1961. 20-plus years had flown by, and yet the event was still fresh and vivid in her memory as if it had occurred yesterday. And in those years, both the young teacher and the United States space program had also come a long way.

Activities at NASA frequently made headlines. Americans were most familiar with the launchings from the Kennedy Space Center north of Cape Canaveral, Florida. But the Johnson Space Center in Houston, Texas, took care of the space flights after liftoff, while the Jet Propulsion Laboratory in Pasadena charted deep space and explored the planets.

Modern spaceflight looked different too. Gone were the exaggerated space suits of past decades with Astronauts in bulky outfits bumping around and topped off by giant bubbled helmets. Now Astronauts donned sleek fitting uniforms that were easy to move in and fully equipped for maximum protection and comfort. Meals aboard the spacecrafts had also changed; gone were miniature food cubes and meals in a pouch, replaced with full-course dinners with a variety of cuisines. Add to that the regularity of missions humanized space travel, and more Americans now saw Astronauts as just people who were willing to train and work hard rather than super-humans who acted much like space robots.

In June 1983, the American space program made another major breakthrough, and Sally Ride became the first American woman to orbit the Earth. "I hope I'm the first of many women to enjoy this experience," Ride said from the Space Shuttle as it glided smoothly across the Earth 150 miles straight up at more than 17,000 MPH.

Government officials sensed the growing public waning interest in the space program, and more projects were set up to encourage citizen participation. However, additional funding was needed to finance the missions, and public support was essential so the tax money could be allotted. Up to this point, only trained astronauts had been sent into space, but the government began toying with the idea of including ordinary citizens on flights.

President Ronald Reagan knew he wanted to send a regular citizen into space, but he didn't want it to be just anyone. In August 1984, the President declared, "I am directing NASA to begin a search in all of our Elementary and Secondary Schools to choose, as the first civilian passenger in the history of our space programs will be one of America's finest… a teacher!"

President Reagan's directive swiftly circulated through all the nooks and crannies of the American government and the world of academia. The NASA Teacher in Space Program became a reality. In Concord, New Hampshire, a 36-year-old teacher and mother pondered all the possibilities.

CHAPTER 6

Space: *The Ultimate Field Trip!*

*"All adventures especially
into new territory, are scary."*
Astronaut Sally Ride.

*"Some say that we should stop exploring space, that the
cost in human lives is too great. But Challenger's crew
would not have wanted that. We are a curious species,
always wanting to know what is over the next hill,
around the next corner, on the next island."*
Stuart Atkinson, Astronomer

No matter how hard Christa tried to put the thought of
becoming the first teacher in space from her mind, it
kept coming back. Steve wasn't about to stand in the
way; in fact, he was encouraging and very proud of her.
"This is what you've wanted for a long time now, and
you've got the chance, so… go for it, baby!" he told her.
McAuliffe considered this to be the chance at the
ultimate field trip, but she knew the competition was to
be fierce. She got busy.

Christa got the NASA application and studied the 25-
page document closely. The basic requirements seemed
simple enough: applicants must be US citizens and
credentialed teachers with at least five years of
experience, they also had to be in good physical and
mental health, have adequate vision, and perhaps most
importantly for Christa, she discovered that the contact

lenses she wore would pose no problem to her ambitions for space travel.

But NASA's essay questions were not so easy. "Describe your teaching philosophy" was a simple one. Christa knew her teaching philosophy well: "Students should be actively involved in learning!" Yet that was only one sentence, and the judges would surely want more. "Why do you want to be the first Teacher In Space?" Answering that question would take a lot of thought. Slowly, Christa filled out the application. She wrote about the thrill of watching Alan Shepard when she was in junior high school and that the space program had always fascinated her.

"I told them how excited I would be to go into space and how thrilled I was when Alan Shepard made his historic flight, and when John Kennedy announced the news that men had landed safely on the Moon, and how jealous I was of those men," McAuliffe said. Christa also emphasized how important she believed it was to have a lay person, a"civilian" traveling in space, and if selected, she promised to keep a complete public diary about all aspects of her training and the mission.

McAuliffe's hope was to humanize the space program, making it clear to the average person, especially young people, what the program means to Americans and all humanity.

Christa was sure students could read her diary and see that any ordinary person could contribute to history. "If they can make that connection, they're going to get excited about history and about the future," said the young educator. For almost two weeks, Christa worked on the application forms every single night. February 1, 1985, was the deadline date circled in red on the kitchen calendar. As cold winter breezes whipped the McAuliffe home in Concord, the high school teacher sipped hot tea and examined her written thoughts. However, as always, her ears were always hyper-alert for any noise from her sleeping children, Caroline and Scott. As she focused on the newspapers covering the table before her, she wrote and rewrote her answers. It was hard work. She had searched her mind, her heart, and her soul for the right answers. She felt more than ready to take her shot.

As a teacher, Christa always tried to make her students feel that they were part of a huge family and that Earth was indeed one gigantic global village. According to her, people had to get along with others to make it all work. McAuliffe felt that seeing the Earth from a spaceship without any physical boundaries could have a profound effect on people. She found the easiest part of the application dealt with the question of "why is it _____ important for a teacher to fly in space?" Christa wrote, "Space is the future, and if as teachers we don't prepare students for the future, we're not doing our jobs, we have to include it."

Although McAuliffe was sure she didn't really have a chance of being selected as the first 'Teacher in Space', she told her classes about the program. "I just want you to try. I just want you to know that it's important that you try," she explained. "We preach and teach it so often in our classrooms that it would be pure hypocrisy not to

HIGH FLIGHT

Oh! I have slipped the surly bonds of Earth
And danced the skies on laughter-silvered wings;
Sunward I've climbed,
and joined the tumbling mirth
Of sun-split clouds, – and done a hundred things
you have not dreamed of –
wheeled and soared and swung
high in the sunlit silence. Hovering there,
I've chased the shouting wind along, and flung
my eager craft through footless halls of air...
Up, up the long, delirious burning blue
I've topped the wind-swept heights
with easy grace
Where never lark, or ever eagle flew –
And, while with silent, lifting mind I've trod
The high untrespassed sanctity of space,
Put out my hand, and touched... the face of God.

John Gillespie Magee

make a strong effort myself. Anyway, my Dad always said, 'some people never fail… but sadly some never try'."

Christa must have re-wrote her NASA application at least five times. Finally, on the morning of February 1, she slipped the forms into a large envelope and dropped it into the mailbox at her local post office around the corner. Christa scolded herself, remembering how many times she has done so to her students about waiting until the last minute to complete their assignments!

She was now in the running, but so were 11,000 other teachers from across the country. Not only did teachers apply from every state in the union, applications also came in from everywhere…Washington DC, Puerto Rico, the Virgin Islands, Guam, and even the Bureau of Indian Affairs. It was going to be tough.

The screening process was intense. Clerks tossed out candidates who failed to meet the initial eligibility requirements, then passed on the remaining applications to state school officials who had to help cull the applicants. Only the top 10 candidates would be reviewed by NASA officials. 79 teachers in New Hampshire applied for the 'Teacher in Space' program, and carefully the list was trimmed. On September 16, 1985, seven teachers in the state gathered at Walker Elementary school in Concord for final interviews, and a nervous teacher Christa McAuliffe was one.

"I was only a mile away from my home and a block away from my church," Christa recalled. "Somehow, that realization gave me a special kind of confidence." That confidence, coupled with sincerity and warmth, gave Christa the extra sparkle she needed to impress the review committee.

Some of the teachers had better resumes, observed Dr. William Everett Sherman to the state selection committee. "But I think when you look at it, Christa was a candidate who could make the most of the opportunity; she had that girl-next-door quality, a kind of wholesome American look, and she was articulate," he said. Most of all, she was a great teacher. "If I can get some student interested in science, if I can show members of the general public what's going on up there in the space program, then my job's been done," McAuliffe said enthusiastically.

Step-by-step Christa inched her way along the selection process. Not feeling confident about herself before the video camera, she practiced in front of a mirror and with a friend's setup. How she looked on tape could play a big role in the final selection.

She began paying more attention to her make-up and clothing and gave extra care in the way she spoke and presented herself while the cameras rolled. When she was being interviewed, McAuliffe described her overall world view: "I have a vision of the world as a global village, a world without boundaries," she said. And she described the diary she would keep in outer space and how this mission could emphasize the importance written records play in overall history. "My job in space will be to observe and write a public journal," she said.

"I'm also going to be teaching a class for students on earth about life in space and about the space shuttle. We'll be conducting some experiments, and I will also have a one-hour program called 'Mission Watch,' where I'll describe details of the mission and give additional information about the trip." She sounded natural, self-assured, and confident, so off the videos went to NASA with fingers crossed and prayers said.

Christa tried to put the competition out of her mind. After all, she had high school students to consider, and as the final weeks of the semester counted down, there were plenty of tests to give, projects to evaluate, and papers to grade. While a busy teacher carefully examined her students' work at Concord High, she was being evaluated by NASA officials. Every word of her application form was scrutinized and her videotape watched several times. Fortunately, she passed with flying colors in every sense of the word, and in June 1985, she was among 114 finalists from across the USA to be invited to Washington DC.

For five days, Christa and other applicants for the new NASA Teacher in Space program met with a national review panel. Questions flowed one after the other, and the answers were pondered by the judges. At this level, all the candidates sounded good, but the group had to be narrowed down to only 10. It was an exhausted Christa who returned home on June 27, 1985. "How do you feel?" Steve asked. Christa shook her head and smiled, "Please don't ask me one more question. I just don't have any answers left," she smiled. Again Christa tried to push the space program out of her mind, it was summertime in the Northeast after all, but when the news arrived that she was one of the Top 10 finalists, Christa couldn't control herself, and her shouts of joy echoed throughout all of New England! Family and friends whispered when speaking of any concerns around Christa… no one wanted to make her any more nervous than she already seemed to be.

On July 7, 1985, the 10 finalists traveled to the Johnson Space Center in Houston, Texas. The final selection rested with the NASA evaluation committee. In the days that followed, each candidate went through a barrage of medical exams, physical and psychological fitness tests as well as lectures about space flight. Christa ran on the treadmill, instruments recording every reaction to the exercises. She tested her strength on space-age muscle-building machines pulling, pushing, lifting, and bending her every which way. Doctors measured every action and reaction. "They found muscles I didn't even know I had!" Christa laughed. She was in great shape.

The goal was to ensure that whoever climbed into that spacecraft for the mission was fully ready and did not suffer from anything like claustrophobia or motion sickness and to make sure all the finalists could stand the extended confinement. One test to explore that was that each applicant was rolled into a 34-inch fabric bag that zipped up from the outside. For 10 minutes, they had to stay inside. Of all the tests, Christa hated this one the most, but she was able to master it and overcome her fears.

The tests continued; the Altitude Test Chamber showed the finalists how to deal with a lack of oxygen in flight, and in a special NASA-designed airplane labeled "The Vomit Comet", candidates experienced short periods of total weightlessness. The plane flies to high altitude and then dives towards the earth, during which passengers experience weightlessness. McAuliffe did just fine.

Once the Houston tests were completed, it was back to Washington DC, where a final group of seven NASA judges put the 10 candidates through one last set of interviews. "I cannot join the space program and restart my life as an astronaut, but I can use this opportunity to connect my abilities as an educator with my interests in history, and space is a unique opportunity to fulfill my early fantasies," she told the Judges. "Space is for everybody. It's not just for a few people in science or math or for a select group of astronauts. That's all of our new frontier out there, and it's everybody's business to know about space." Two of the 10 contenders would be selected: a winner as well as a runner-up, and both would go through the complete NASA training program.

"You have to dream. We all have to dream. Dreaming is OK. Imagine me teaching from space, all over the world, touching so many people's lives. That's a teacher's dream! I have a vision of the world as a global village, a world without boundaries. Imagine a history teacher making history!"

On July 19, 1985, the Roosevelt Room at the White House was crowded with news media, and it was wall-to-wall people. They were all on hand for the official

announcement as to which of the 10 assembled
candidates was going into space. Vice President George
Bush Sr., a big supporter of the space program and a
former WWII aviator, stepped forward to the
microphone, and the room hushed. Carefully, the Vice
President traced the procedures for selecting the teacher
with "Just the right stuff!" Bush smiled, "I thought I was
the world traveler, but this one tops anything I've ever
tried!" The 10 candidates stood nervously behind him.
Moving the program along, Vice President Bush
announced the first runner-up to be Barbara Morgan, a
second-grade teacher from McCall, Idaho. If the first
choice couldn't go, Mrs. Morgan would. Then the Vice
President said that the first Teacher in Space would be…
Christa McAuliffe!

Bush cheerfully handed Christa a beautiful trophy
picturing a student gazing up at a teacher who is
pointing to the stars. Dazed and teary-eyed, Christa
moved toward the microphone. She had to fight for the

right words, "It's not often that a teacher is at a loss of words," Christa acknowledged with a smile, "I know my students wouldn't think so. I've made nine wonderful friends over the last two weeks," she continued, pausing to look at the other teachers, "and when that shuttle goes, there might be one body, but there's gonna be 10 souls that I'm taking with me. Thank you!" As people applauded, Christa stepped back and nodded her appreciation. She was sure all of this was just a dream and that any moment she'd be waking up.

CHAPTER 7
73 Seconds

*"I really don't want to say goodbye
to any of you people."*
Christa McAuliffe

*"My God, Thiokol,
when do ya want me to launch? Next April?!"*
Lawrence Mulloy, NASA Marshall Spaceflight Center
Jan. 27, 1986

This was not a dream. Christa Corrigan McAuliffe, 37, a simple history teacher from Concord, Massachusetts, was to be the first United States civilian in space, and it just so happened that she was also a teacher. If you didn't know that on July 19, 1985, you hadn't read a newspaper nor watched or listened to a news broadcast. People around the world came to recognize Christa's picture overnight, and everyone was talking about how she had been selected and how exciting it all was.

But in the town of Concord, New Hampshire, Christa was just one of their own, and plans flew into motion for an official "Christa McAuliffe Day". However, it couldn't be held right away because first, Christa had to make guest appearances on national television and radio shows like the Tonight Show. On the show, Johnny Carson drew loud laughter when he remarked that he would like to send a few of his past teachers into space. "But you don't really seem like one of those," Carson told Christa with a wink.

Later, when Christa appeared before the National Education Association's annual convention, teachers from around the country gave her a standing ovation. "We couldn't have settled on a better choice," organization officials said, "she will be a great spokesperson for our profession," was the consensus.

Returning home, Christa enjoyed a day in her honor, smiling and waving as she rode in a convertible down the town's main street. It was as if she was the Homecoming Queen. The major events on Christa McAuliffe Day, August 6, 1985, included her signing autographs and greeting hundreds of well-wishers. She even directed the school band playing 'Stars and Stripes Forever' as the McAuliffe family looked on. Seven-year-old son Scott remarked that it was 'cool' having a mom like his, while Caroline was still too young to appreciate everything happening.

One thing was certain, She was going to miss her students while she was gone, that was sure. "It was hard telling those kids… that I wasn't going to be there this year. And I knew I was going to miss them," McAuliffe said. "I won't have an opportunity to see them again unless they stop by the house. Now during the summer, I got lots of notes; kids would stop by the house. I'd be pulling weeds or something, and they would come up and give me a hug and say, 'Oh, I can't believe it, this is so wonderful!' and just get very excited about it," she said. "And I have found that it is difficult for me not being in school teaching."

Once the television lights dimmed a bit and the music subsided… it was time for Christa to actively begin her preparation for flight. Meanwhile, a new history teacher would sit behind Christa's desk at Concord High School for the 1985-86 school year. In September, Christa headed back to Houston in preparation for a space mission that would be strenuous both physically and mentally.

But most of all, she worried more about what the Challenger astronauts would think of her. After all, they were trained professionals… how would they feel towards an outsider? How would someone who specializes in chalkboards and seating charts, not rocket engines and telemetry, fit into this elite group of professional individuals who had trained forever?

Christa's fears were soon put to rest, and from the first encounter with her future cabin mates, she was made to feel like one of them. "I was a little concerned with how the crew was going to view me because I didn't know whether this program had been kinda forced down their throats or not. But they were really wonderful," she explained. Together they laughed, joked around, and sometimes, they called Christa "Teach". She felt a special kinship with Teacher in Space runner-up Barbara Morgan and with NASA Mission Specialist Judy Resnick, the first Jewish Astronaut. Together with Morgan, Resnick was the only other female member of the crew, and there was an immediate bond between the three women.

The other team members were also the best of the very best of NASA:

Commander Francis Dick Scobee knew Christa's contributions to the mission would be important. "Ours will be known as 'The Teacher Mission', which is fine," he said. "People will remember what we do." The team leader, who came from Washington state, was 46 years old, a Vietnam vet, and had flown over 45 different kinds of aircraft.

Mission Specialist Ronald McNair, 36, was a North Carolina native who earned a Doctorate in Physics from the Massachusetts Institute of Technology in 1984. Previously, he had launched a multi-million dollar communication satellite from the Shuttle.

Shuttle Pilot Michael Smith, 40, also came from North Carolina. He was a Vietnam vet who had joined the NASA space program in 1980.

Astronaut Greg Jarvis was an electrical engineer originally from Detroit, Michigan. He served four years in the Air Force before working for Hughes Aircraft as a satellite designer. He was 41.

Fellow mission STS-51L team member, 39-year-old Ellison S. Onizuka, was an aeronautical space engineer from Hawaii. After earning degrees at the University of Colorado, Allison had worked as a test pilot and flight engineer for the United States Air Force. He joined the space program in 1978.

Together, it was a superior and synergistic team that was 110% mission-ready. Comfortable with her new NASA teammates Christa focused on the work ahead. The pre-launch training program included advanced lectures and body conditioning that would kill most.

65

From the moment of her arrival, Christa slipped into a rigid schedule… the daytime hours focused on physical activity and working with a fully equipped model of the Shuttle. They walked through almost every aspect of the mission. They had to know how to handle all the controls, do their experiments and how to eat, how to sleep and even how to go to the bathroom, all while in space. The weightless factor made everything more complicated. It was essential that the crew knew how to fully operate the craft to get the most out of the mission and also just in case something was to go wrong up there.

Christa remembered how each summer her students complained about how many books they had to carry and how heavy they were… if only those same students could've seen the manuals and textbooks she had to haul. "I think if they were stacked up, they might be taller than the Challenger itself!" Christa joked. The daily workout sessions, the training evolutions, and the nightly study routine drained much of Christa's energy, and she sometimes wondered if she was doing the right thing. She would never show it. And Christa knew that there were also people in Concord who felt she had no business taking part in a space mission— after all, didn't she have a husband and two children to care for?

But Steve would miss his wife. "Christa's absence simply gives me a chance to do some things I probably should've learned to do anyway," he declared. "A man can cook, keep house and look after his kids. I may not do it as well as my wife, but I'll sure try." When Christa heard, she said, "I really married a great guy!"

McAuliffe carefully planned the extra duties she would carry out during the mission. She would teach as she often did, but this time, her students would be on earth while she flew approximately 150 miles above them. She would lead them in the ultimate field trip, and this one would take students watching via close circuit television for a tour around the space shuttle, while another lesson would highlight the past, present, and future of space missions and space flight in general. Each lesson would run for about 15 minutes. When she talked about teaching in the spacecraft, her voice became animated. There was no doubt whatsoever that Christa looked forward to teaching from the Challenger platform in Space.

In October, Christa got a break from the intense training and study schedule as she and Steve were invited to the White House as special guests. For the history teacher from Concord, the evening of dinner and dancing held a special significance. "I guess I'm always looking for the historical perspective," Christa laughed, "you can bet I'll be putting this one into the journal for sure!" And she did.

It was also in October that Christa got her first close look at the Challenger spacecraft. Seeing it upfront was a whole new experience. It was huge. The spacecraft measures 122 feet long with a wingspan of 78 feet, weighing in at more than 4.6 million pounds. The two problematic Solid Rocket Boosters (SRB) had 11

separate segments. The SRB was huge at 3-4 meters around and was almost the length of the entire shuttle. The SRBs burn at 3200 degrees for only about 2 minutes, producing 3.3 million pounds of thrust. Once spent, they are released via explosive bolts, fall back to the sea, and are then retrieved for re-use. In theory and in practice it was a cumbersome but cost effective way to get to space.

In the Shuttle's 40 years of amazing service, 135 missions flew 355 Astronauts on the 5 Shuttle Orbiters that were built at a cost of about $5.5 Billion. Cost per launch/mission was approximately $1.2 billion. Once ready, it was brought to the launchpad and then sat like a proud white bird ready for flight. At night, the spotlights on the Spacecraft made for a special sight and could be seen for many miles away.

To the outside world, it sometimes appeared as if Christa was having too much fun during training and getting ready for the shuttle mission. She folded her hands and did a Russian cossack dance in the weightless cabin of the KC 135 'Vomit Comet', and news clips showed McAuliffe and Morgan playing leapfrog. It made a few people scratch their heads in wonderment… was this all just a game? Hardly. It was a serious game of chance that was being played,
NASA had 'Go Fever' and a hectic schedule to keep. A total of 15 space shuttle missions were planned for 1986, more than one a month, and the Challenger would be the first for that year. The craft had flown on 9 previous flights before mission STS-51L.

The Astronauts and the entire NASA team took mission STS-51L very seriously, and the moments of fun and relaxation were few and far between. But it was felt they were sorely needed to release the pent-up nervous energy which would take its toll on anyone connected with the mission if they allowed it.

For most people, a countdown begins ten seconds before a spacecraft lifts off from the launch pad but not for the Astronauts and the NASA team. Their countdown begins months before lift off and each day of preparation is carefully planned and very important. There was so much to do and so many details to check; nothing was ever done just once. Everything had to be checked and rechecked. Safety was always uppermost in their minds and they trained to prepare the Flight team to handle any possible mission contingencies or launch emergencies.

McAuliffe's return to Concord for Thanksgiving in November 1985 was quiet and uneventful. Between bites of turkey and dressing, she made plans with her family and friends about who would be coming to Houston in January for the launch. Christa's son Scott was especially proud of his Mom, who promised to take his special stuffed toy Frog with her into space.

They also made arrangements to take Scott's entire third-grade class down to the Cape to witness the launch. Between Thanksgiving and Christmas, Christa returned to Houston to make final preparations for the mission. Christmas that year was very special in the McAuliffe household. It was time for everyone who ever knew Christa Corrigan McAuliffe to meet her in person, by card, or by telephone to wish her a safe flight. In less than a month, she would make history.

As the McAuliffe family attended mass in Concord during the holidays, the Priest of the parish offered special prayers that God would take good care of his beloved servant Christa. She was touched, and she remarked to her friends that she felt especially close to God at this time in her life. She also commented that when she was flying in the clouds, she felt that way. Once back in Houston, all attention focused on the scheduled launch date of January 22, and again, everything was repeated, and every detail was double-checked. Nothing would be left to chance.

When the January 22 launch was scrubbed because of scheduling problems, there was little surprise. Delays were common in the history of the space program. A second delay occurred when a dust storm was predicted for an emergency landing site half a world away, and strong wind and rain canceled the next attempt. By the third attempt to launch, frustration was beginning to show among the Challenger crew and flight team. Some of the McAuliffe's friends who had made the trip to Texas had to return home. And it was always comparatively small glitches that prevented flight; on January 27, it was a hatch latch on the door that prevented the spacecraft from going up. "We're definitely eager to go," Christa said. She and the other crew would soon get their chance.

The morning of January 28 was gorgeously clear and cold. The temperature stopped climbing at only 24°, and icicles sparkling in the morning sunlight trimmed the Challenger spacecraft sitting on the pad. When Christa joined the other six astronauts for a 7 AM preflight breakfast, the chatter was upbeat and cheerful. They were definitely going up today!

Photographers outside the operations buildings yelled out, "How do you feel, Christa?!" as the Challenger crew emerged."I feel great!" she shot back, waving and smiling on her way to the pad. For NASA, she was a PR godsend. In the Launch Control Center, four miles from the blastoff spot, Steve, Scott, and Caroline McAuliffe waited with the other members of the Astronauts' immediate families. Grace and Ed Corrigan, Christa's Mom and Dad, were not considered members of the immediate family, so they had to wait where other VIPs gathered outside.

Across the country, at Concord High School in New Hampshire, 1200 students settled into their chairs before television sets throughout the building. Many wore T-shirts that read "Concorde… Where the spirit is high!" or "Go Christa Go!" When a micro switch failed inside the spacecraft, technicians tried to fix it, and then there were problems with the door handle, so a power drill and a hacksaw were called for. It seemed as if the shuttle itself was trying to stall the launch!

While the NASA ground crew struggled to correct the 'Hold', minutes slipped into hours, and both the crowds below and the crew, laying on their backs in full spacesuits, grew restless and annoyed. "I feel like going in there and getting her off the ground myself!" grumbled Mr. Corrigan. "She wouldn't come," his wife responded. Mrs. Corrigan shivered inside her white coat, pulling its fluffy collar tightly around her neck to protect herself from the near-freezing temperatures. Somehow she had a bad feeling about this, and things just didn't seem right… she couldn't explain it, she would recall later.

Finally, with the minor troubles addressed, the repair team exited the pad, leaving the Challenger crew alone to continue their last-minute preparations as they sat on top of what could safely be called a large bomb. The count-down clock resumed. T-minus 3 minutes! Testing the headsets, Mission Control spoke to each of the Astronauts. "Hope we go today!" they said to Christa; "Hope so too!" she answered. Those were her last recorded words on earth.

The final hold was over, people took their positions, and their attention focused on the launching site as a voice over the loudspeaker began counting down"10, 9, 8, 7..." Spectators joined in, "6, 5, 4, 3, 2, 2... lift off!" they all shouted. The ignited rockets thundered and shook the space center and the entire ground. As everything trembled slowly, ever so slowly, the giant white metal bird rose past the tower. It thrust across the morning sky as the icicles that covered it disintegrated. Inside the space center, outside on the bleachers, and in the classrooms of Concord high school and across America, people broke into cheers. Americans were certainly cheering for the astronauts, for Christa, and for NASA, but they were also cheering somehow for themselves and in the pride they felt in their nation and what it could do. Faster and faster, now at 1000 miles an hour, the Challenger shuttle climbed into the sky very very slowly at first...10,000 feet, 15,000 feet,

20,000 feet, the rocket's fire at the base of the white cylinder glowed brightly against the azure blue canvas of sky… it was a picture perfect scene. No one noticed at the time the small area of smoke and eventual fire on the lower right side of the starboard SRB booster rocket. At 60 seconds into the launch ground control ordered "go throttle up!" This was the command to open the engines and give them full power. Alert Commander Scoby responded "Roger, go with throttle up." No sooner had Scoby echo the command then Pilot Smith's voice came from the Challenger… "Uh Oh!" At 73 seconds on the mission clock the shuttle was engulfed in flames experiencing a 'catastrophic incident' and a 'major malfunction'.

Smith, the Pilot, was probably the only crew member who had a fraction of a second to see the orange flash on the rocket booster and realize what it was. In the next instant the large external fuel tank exploded wrapping the entire spacecraft in fire. The Challenger split into 1000 pieces hurling wreckage in every direction. The nightmare some had predicted was coming true.

The people below and those watching on television really couldn't believe what they were seeing. The Shuttle Challenger had exploded less than two minutes into flight. From an altitude of 70,000 feet parts of the spacecraft drifted down like confetti into the Atlantic ocean. It was over … it was all over.

CHAPTER 8

Aftermath & Legacy

On January 28, 1986 shock and trauma spread across our country, the depth of the nation's grief was impossible to measure. From the bus driver to the doctor to the store keeper, everyone was affected to some degree and many showed it. There are marker stones in our lives when events happened that we will always remember; Kennedy and King assassinations, the striking of the towers on 9/11, this was one of those moments. Older people compared it to the tragic November afternoon in 1963 when President Kennedy was assassinated. The thought of seven Americans full of life and energy cut down as they attempted to open another door to space travel was hard for most Americans to accept. This was especially true given NASA's many successes and the special nature of the 'Teacher in Space' mission. It was more than a tragedy.

The death of the first private citizen on a space mission, a wife and mother of two young children, was especially horrific. Christa did everything with such a sense of joy and wonder that it was a real loss to anyone with a heart. President Reagan who introduced the idea of a teacher in space, was grief stricken and he postponed the State of the Union address he was to give before Congress that night. The speech was delayed and a national week of mourning for the Challenger crew was declared. At the memorial service held the next week at the Johnson Space Center in

Houston, President Reagan said that the brave space travelers aboard the Challenger had "slipped the surly bonds of earth to touch the face of God." There was a real human element to this tragedy…

At Concord High School, traumatized students, teachers, and alumni packed into the school gym for their own memorial service. It was nothing swanky, just hometown people giving tribute to one of their own. They sang songs, read poetry she liked, and recalled many of Mrs. McAuliffe's favorite sayings and stories about the popular teacher. A dry eye was not to be found anywhere.

It took almost six months before investigators determined the cause of the Challenger tragedy officially, but it was obvious almost immediately to veteran onlookers. An O-ring on the Solid Rocket Booster had failed. The cold weather caused a gap in the seal between one of the 11 segments, and when the seal opened, flames escaped, and that led to the fatal explosion. And it was not the first time.

It was something NASA had been warned about since the second space shuttle launch when 'Blow By' was discovered in SRB post-flight analysis. Each section of the SRB has 'O' rings that help seal the sections together. When it's cold outside, the rings become brittle and so do not form nor maintain a proper seal. That's a real problem, but it was not one that was unknown. It was ignored, perhaps, but as early as the second mission, engineers had warned of the problem and said it was just a matter of time before NASA ran out of luck and killed some very fine people.

In five of the previous 7 shuttle missions before the Challenger 'accident' there was significant "Blow By" as evidenced by black soot found outside the solid rocket booster near the O-Ring flange. Morton Thiokol warned NASA again in January 1985 after the shuttle launched at 51 degrees.

Teacher in Space Project

In the final analysis, there was plenty of blame and fault to go around. We won't belabor here the fact that Morton Thiokol Industries directly and repeatedly warned NASA officials about their faulty design and that any launch under 53° was ill-advised because of the potential for O-ring failure. To date, Morton Thiokol nor NASA has yet to be charged for what some feel amounts to criminal negligence. The Astronauts' families, some of whom sued both organizations, reached a financial settlement of some sort and were required to sign legal non-disclosure agreements, ensuring that we will perhaps never know if real accountability of some sort ever occurred.

Another thing that is also not really talked about, at least with enough emphasis, is ice. The shuttle was covered with it that morning. It had been documented on previous occasions that anything striking the surface of the shuttle was ill-advised, and yet NASA officials seemed unconcerned about the potential for ice strikes on the shuttle.

The fact is that at the time, the Reagan administration had been involved in several illicit scandals like Iran Contra, and the Administration was anxious to turn the page and provide the American people with something positive. They wanted the President to speak with the Shuttle Crew in space from the floor of the Congress during the State of the Union address.

At the time, NASA was all about "Affordable and reliable transportation to and from space, on time and on budget!" That was a direct quote from the agency. "It's about the Launch Schedule. Our job is to launch… on time, every time," was another. The political pressure from the Administration and its clients like the US Air Force to maintain its flight schedule was significant. Outsiders call this "Go Fever", and it is a disease that had the NASA organization firmly in its grips at the time. Sadly, "full safety" took a back seat while "acceptable risk" got in the driver's seat and sped off to a dangerous future.

There are three main discrepancies to the current official story of the Challenger disaster and what transpired. One is NASA's general policy of 'no comment' when it comes to the Astronauts and the accident. The agency has always suffered from an overall lack of transparency and has never been forthcoming when it comes to their failures or shortcomings, not with the Media, the

American public, or with Congress. In the aftermath, NASA reached financial settlements with the Astronauts' families and made them sign Non-disclosure Agreements so that the true story may never be told. The second aspect is that there is every indication that the shuttle astronauts survived the initial explosions, and they were alive as the crew cabin fell to earth for almost 3 minutes, hitting the cement-hard Atlantic at 207 MPH, instantly killing all aboard who may have been alive. The Crew cabin came to rest in 100' of water about 18 nautical miles east of launch pad 39B from whence it came. It took the US Navy several weeks to find and recover the bodies and the wreckage. And perhaps the third most important aspect of the incident, and one that is often overlooked, is the fact that technologies existed, both then and now, that would have and could have given the crew a much better-than-average chance at survival. Sadly, we may never really know the full true story, but it is clear that there is more to be revealed by NASA and Morton Thiokol. With the evidence at hand, the Author feels we simply cannot in good conscience call this an 'accident'. This is not a new nor unpopular sentiment.

Perhaps the final congressional Rodgers Report summed it up most succinctly: "When Challenger broke up, it was traveling at 1.9 times the speed of sound at an altitude of 48,000 feet. The crew module continued flying upward for some 25 seconds to an altitude of about 65,000 feet before beginning the long fall to the ocean. From breakup to impact took two minutes and 45 seconds. Impact velocity was 207 mph, subjecting the module to a braking force of approximately 200 times the force of gravity. Any astronauts (alive) were killed instantly," he said.

Dr. Joseph Kerwin, Director of Space and Life Sciences at the Johnson Space Center, added in his final report: "The forces on the orbiter (shuttle) at breakup were probably too low to cause death or serious injury… the crew possibly, but not certainly, lost consciousness in the seconds following orbiter breakup. The maximum acceleration forces felt by the astronauts as their cabin was blown away from the explosion—estimated at 12 to 20 Gs, or 12 to 20 times the force of gravity—were quite brief," Kerwin added, and that they were indeed "survivable". Even if the sealed crew compartment had ruptured and depressurized," he said at a news conference, "the crew could have remained conscious for 6 to 15 seconds. If the cabin remained intact, though, they may have been conscious for nearly three terrifying minutes--as upward momentum carried the cabin from 48,000 ft. at the moment of the fireball to 65,000 ft. 25 seconds later, before it fell, tumbling and spinning, and crashed into the waves at 207 mph. with a force of about 200 Gs." Hindsight is always 20/20, but even a blind man can see that this is a tragedy that was foretold, warned about, and simply didn't need to happen and there is more than enough blame to go around. As we go back to the Moon… lessons learned.

As a silver lining to all this, Christa lives on in various organizations that carry on her advocacy and legacy. In the years since the mission in 1986, teacher and educational organizations have memorialized McAuliffe and invoked her life to encourage students' interest in STEM (Science, Technology, Engineering, Mathematics) education. Many of McAuliffe's former students went on to become teachers themselves, inspired by her life and passion for education.

The popular Space Camp is another example of Christa's impact!

Foremost among these organizations is 'Challenger Center' and its 'Learning Centers' across the country. It is a 501c3 nonprofit organization and the Challenger Learning Centers are all independent of the larger organization.

As a leader in STEM education, The Challenger Center and its network of Challenger Learning

Centers across the nation provide more than 250,000 students annually with experiential education programs to engage students in real and innovative hands-on learning opportunities. The goal is to show young students that people are natural explorers and innovators, and that if they become involved in STEM educational opportunities they will make the connection that if they work hard a career in the space industry is a real possibility.

A recent Center alum summed it up perfectly; "Challenger Center inspires kids to dream big. To me, the adventures of people like Neil Armstrong, Buzz Aldrin, and Dick Scobee were so far away, without Challenger Center, I would have never believed that a kid like me could be anything like them."

These programs strengthen knowledge in STEM subjects and inspire students to pursue careers in these important fields. Founded in 1986, the organization was created to honor the seven astronauts of shuttle flight STS-51-L. Challenger Centers are non-profit and are worthy of your support. To donate or learn more about Challenger Centers, please visit:

www.challenger.org

Elsewhere, The Christa McAuliffe Center in New Hampshire features a regular schedule of teacher workshops and a children's planetarium. Additionally, the New Hampshire Education Department and other educational organizations annually sponsor special

scholarships in the name of Christa McAuliffe and most are destined for students who want to become teachers. And these are only some of the many organizations that continue the vital work of helping students and future teachers... to reach for the stars!

In 2007, Astronaut Teacher Barbara Morgan finally continued the 'Teacher In Space' program and became the first teacher to successfully fly on the shuttle into space. The official examination of the accident has ended, but independent investigations are still ongoing even after all these years. Perhaps someday, we will learn the truth. Christa and company are due that. There's no doubt that Christa McAuliffe left an indelible mark on the world. Her adventurous and inquisitive spirit lives on, particularly in those who touch the lives of students. All these various organizations help her legacy live on.

With her faith in God, her love for her family and the nation, McAuliffe reached beyond the clouds towards the stars. "You'll never know what you can really do until you try! Ordinary people *can* do extraordinary things," Christa often said. She proved that she was right, and her lessons and life will never be forgotten.

Weather
Today ...

The Washington Post

FINAL

109TH YEAR · · · No. 55 · · · WEDNESDAY, JANUARY 29, 1986 · · · 25¢

Space Shuttle Explodes, Killing Crew

Fire Engulfs Ship With 7 Aboard Soon After Liftoff

By Boyce Rensberger
Washington Post Staff Writer

The space shuttle Challenger, carrying six astronauts and schoolteacher Christa McAuliffe, exploded in a burst of fire 74 seconds after liftoff yesterday, killing all seven aboard and stunning a world made witness to the event by television.

The unexplained explosion occurred without warning as the flight seemed to be proceeding flawlessly at about 2,000 feet per second, 10 miles above Earth and eight miles down range from Cape Canaveral. The spacecraft appeared to disintegrate into bits of debris that rained into the Atlantic Ocean. Those aboard, still strapped into their seats, had no means of escape.

In addition to McAuliffe, those killed were spacecraft commander Francis R. (Dick) Scobee, Navy Cmdr. Michael J. Smith, mission specialist Judith A. Resnik, mission specialist Ronald E. McNair, Air Force Lt. Col. Ellison S. Onizuka, and payload specialist Gregory B. Jarvis.

It was the worst accident in the history of space exploration and the first time anyone has been killed during an American space flight. The tragedy occurred 19 years and one day after U.S. astronauts Virgil I. (Gus) Grissom, Roger A. Chaffee and Edward H. White died during a training session when a fire broke out in their sealed Apollo spacecraft on the launch pad.

Five hours after yesterday's tragedy, Jesse W. Moore, associate administrator for space flight of the National Aeronautics and Space Administration, announced from Cape Canaveral that the shuttle program had been suspended for an exhaustive investigation. But President Reagan, who postponed his State of the Union speech from last night to next Tuesday, vowed in a nationally televised statement from the Oval Office that exploration of space would continue.

"There will be more shuttle flights and more shuttle crews and, yes, more volunteers, more civilians, more teachers in space," Reagan said. "Nancy and I are pained to the core over the tragedy of the shuttle Challenger. We know we share this

See SHUTTLE, A6, Col. 3

★ Related stories of the shuttle disaster on Pages A4-A16 and B1.

Near the launch site, Christa McAuliffe's sister, left, and parents react during shuttle flight.

Solid rocket boosters veer away from exploded fragments of Challenger and its liquid fuel tank.

Suddenly, the Celebration Stopped
Joy Turns to Grief in Teacher-Astronaut's Town As Students at High School See Tragedy Unfold

By Laura A. Kiernan
Washington Post Staff Writer

CONCORD, N.H., Jan. 28 — "We were rejoicing in the shaft. We were exulting in it. We were celebrating with her. Then it stopped. That's all. It stopped," said Concord High School principal Charles Foley, his voice shaking.

During an emotional news conference this afternoon, Foley stood in the auditorium where, hours before, students with party hats and noisemakers had ushered into stunned silence as they realized, slowly, that the shuttle carrying Concord teacher Christa McAuliffe had exploded.

The horrifying moment when Challenger lifted off gloriously and burst apart was witnessed on television by schoolchildren, fellow workers and families throughout McAu-

liffe's town. The excitement that had swelled here since July when McAuliffe was selected as the first teacher in space turned to shock, and shock to grief.

The flight's terrible miscarriage also evoked resentment from some students toward reporters and camera crews who periodically disrupted their lives over the last six months and made their money a public spectacle today. When the extent of the disaster became clear, a voice on the public address system asked students to return to their classrooms and news people to leave the building.

Dismissed early, some of the departing students declined to give their names, others to speak at all. "It's pretty hard to handle," one boy said.

"It's a terrible, terrible loss for me," Foley

See CONCORD, A9, Col. 1

The Horror Dawned Slowly
For One Very Long Moment After the Explosion, Few Realized They Had Witnessed a Disaster

By Kathy Sawyer
Washington Post Staff Writer

CAPE CANAVERAL, Jan. 28 — Awareness came slowly, not at a brisk burst, to those watching the shuttle launch from the better seats — the grandstands set up for families of the astronauts, dignitaries, the news media and a class of third graders with connections.

The chest-trembling, concussive roar of the liftoff, lagging behind the rising spaceship, had reached us. The spacecraft, climbing fly-fashion to the "well" of tanks containing 3.8 million pounds of fuel, had been up about one minute.

We were gasping and cheering at the column of fire-topped smoke growing like a beanstalk into a cold, blue sky. As the rumbling sound (still trailing the visible scene) continued, a concave counter-tail seemed to form almost gently at the top, with glints of fire in it.

It took an age to realize that the column ended there.

One of the smaller solid rocket boosters could be seen looping out and back to toward the shuttle, trailing smoke. Other trails appeared.

"Obviously, ... a major malfunction," has recurred," the voice of Mission Control, Steve Nesbitt, who normally speaks crisply, said slowly over the NASA public address system.

"They're coming back," said Reader's Digest writer Malcolm McConnell, who has covered 16 launches. He and several other reporters started running, planning to make their way to the landing strip several miles away where the shuttle was to return in an emergency. There were confused shouts.

Then, still looking up, McConnell sat back down. "Where are they?" someone asked. "Dead," he answered flatly. "We've lost 'em, God bless 'em."

See SCENE, A7, Col. 1

CHALLENGER 1986

$75.00 MT

CHRISTA McAULIFFE 1948-1986

MOÇAMBIQUE

NASA

Christa Corrigan McAuliffe
TIMELINE

1948 - Born in Boston Massachusetts

1970 - BS degree, Framingham State College

1970 - Marries Steven McAuliffe

1976 - Gives birth to son Scott

1978 - Master of Science degree from
Bowie State University

1979 - Gives birth to daughter Caroline

1982–1985 - Teacher Concord High School

1985 - NASA's 'Teacher in Space Program'

1986 - Dies in the space shuttle Challenger

2000's - Christa appears on several stamps
and coins from various nations

2004 - Congressional Medal of Honor

2017 - Inducted International Air & Space
Hall of Fame

Challenger STS-51L Crew

•Spacecraft Commander Dick Scobee
Born - May 19, 1939
Birth place - Elum, Washington

•Pilot Michael J. Smith
Born on April 30, 1945
Birth place - Beaufort, North Carolina

•Mission Specialist Judith A. Resnik
Born - April 5, 1949
Birth place - Akron, Ohio

•Mission Specialist Ronald E. McNair
Born - October 21, 1950
Birth place - Lake City, South Carolina

•Mission Specialist Ellison S. Onizuka
Born - June 24, 1946
Birth place - Kona, Hawaii

•Payload Specialist Gregory B. Jarvis
Born - August 24, 1944
Birth place - Detroit, Michigan

•Teacher Christa McAuliffe
NASA Teacher in Space Program
Born - Sept. 2, 1948
Birth place - Boston, MA

Sources & Suggested Reading List

The Space Shuttle by Gregory Voight
Millbrook Press Publishers, 1991

Teacher in Space by Collin Burgess
University of Nebraska Press , 2018

Christa McAuliffe–Pioneer Space Teacher by Charlene Billings
Enslow Publishers, 1986

A Journal for Christa by Grace and George Corrigan
University of Nebraska Press, 1983

"I Touch the Future!" by Robert Holler
Random House, 1986

Christa McAuliffe-Teacher in Space by Rose Blue and Karine Nathan
Millbrook Press Publishers, 1991

The Space Shuttle by Gregory Voight
Millbrook Press Publishers, 1991

Teacher in Space by Collin Burgess
University of Nebraska Press, 2018

Life Magazine - February 1996
"Christa's dream lives on 10 years after"

The Space Shuttle Challenger Disaster: The History and Legacy of
NASA's Most Notorious Tragedy by Charles River
Editors Press, 2010

The Burning Blue: The Untold Story of Christa McAuliffe and NASA's
Challenger Disaster by Kevin Cook
Holt Publishing, 2021

The Rodgers Report: Congressional Investigation into the Challenger
Accident House Report #99-1016
https://www.govinfo.gov/content/pkg/GPO-CRPT-99hrpt1016/pdf/GPO-CRPT-99hrpt1016.pdf

Challenger: The Final Flight': Netflix Video Documentary, 2020

Acknowledgments

NASA - Public & Media Affairs Department

The Challenger Foundation

The McAuliffe Family

The Corrigan Family

Kennedy Space Flight Center, Florida

Johnson Space Flight Center, Houston TX

Space Camp USA

Challenger Centers

The Christa McAuliffe Center

The Washington Post

The Associated Press

Advisor Dale L. Roberts

Advisor Brian Meeks

The Sharon Harvill Foundation

STUDY QUESTIONS

1) What did Christa need to begin Teaching?

2) How fast does the Shuttle need to go for orbit?

3) Where did Christa and Steve listen to the Moon landing?

4) What percentage of thrust does the solid rocket booster provide?

5) How many times had the Challenger flown before?

6) What year was Christa born?

7) How long was the Challenger's Flight?

8) What is the Shuttle's Heat Shield made of?

9) How many children did Christa have?

10) What does STS stand for?

ANSWERS

1. BA in Education and State Credentials, 2. 18,000 MPH, 3. In the car while camping, 4. 71%, 5. Nine times, 6. 1948, 7. 73 seconds, 8. Sand, 9. two, 10. Space Transportation System

<u>NOTES</u>

Books by Author Tom McAuliffe

THE 'McAuliffe' SERIES

• **Mr. Mulligan** - *The Life of Champion Armless Golfer Tommy McAuliffe*

• **Nuts!** - *The Life & Times of General Tony McAuliffe*

• **Throttle Up!** - *Astronaut Teacher Christa McAuliffe*

• **MAD DOG** - *Detroit Tiger Dick McAuliffe*

• **Life of the Party** - *Governor Terry McAuliffe*

Book, eBooks & Audiobooks on sale at Amazon, Kindle, Apple iBooks, Barnes & Noble and your favorite local independent book store!

PLEASE LEAVE US A REVIEW!

Please visit:
WWW.AUTHORTOMMCAULIFFE.COM

Lightning Source UK Ltd.
Milton Keynes UK
UKHW020703060223
416538UK00014B/966